AMMONITE

COLLECTED POEMS

C.E. TRUEMAN

Published by New Generation Publishing in 2017

Copyright © C. E. Trueman 2017

First Edition

The author asserts the moral right under the Copyright, Designs and Patents Act 1988 to be identified as the author of this work.

All Rights reserved. No part of this publication may be reproduced, stored in a retrieval system or transmitted, in any form or by any means without the prior consent of the author, nor be otherwise circulated in any form of binding or cover other than that in which it is published and without a similar condition being imposed on the subsequent purchaser.

www.newgeneration-publishing.com

To my Rosebuds

Contents

AMMONITE 1
SHE SHORE 2
BEYOND THE SENSE OF ROAD 3
OLD STORIES AND NEW ONES 4
CAESAR 5
THE THREAD 6
BOY IN A BOAT 7
KITE SURFER 8
MENISCUS ACROBAT 9
THE PLAYGROUND 10
INDIAN SUMMER 11
AUTUMN FINDINGS 12
BIRDSONG 13
    Robin 13
    Barn Owl 14
    Blackbird 14
    Song Thrush 15
    Starlings 15
    Wren 16
    Pigeons 17
REQUIEM FOR A DAWN CHORUS 18
CORNWALL 19
SELLING THE WIND 20
THE ROSE 21
INSIDE LOVE 22
GLOVES 23
SONG OF THE UNIVERSE 24

SEPTEMBER	25
AFTER THE DINNER PARTY	26
DEATH'S ACRE	27
THE LAST NEGATIVE	28
IN THE BOOKSHOP	29
A VIEW FROM ST MARY'S	30
THE DISAPPEARED	31
STUDY OF A TEARDROP	32
THE SLOW DIVE	33
LITTLE CAGE	34
SUGAR THIEF	35
CANOUAN	36
SLEEPLESSNESS	37
THE ARCHITECT OF MOTHS	38
SKIPPING STONES	39
THE MEMORY OF SNOW	40
FIREWORKS	41
ORIGAMI	42
CHURCHYARD CHILDREN	43
SNOWMAN	44
FINAL NOTES OF A BOY (ON EXPEDITION TO THE CAIRNGORMS)	45
MUNTJAC	46
THE OLDEST TANNERY IN MARRAKECH	47
THE ROUTE TO DA NANG	48
THE SPIRIT'S PLAYHOUSE	49
POPPIES	50

AMMONITE

Cracking the black rock reveals
creation's perfect spiral
that mineral made immortal
named after a god.
Conceived in a tropical sea
made cold by migration,
it gestated in its stone sediment womb
for two hundred millennia.
Like the spun arm of a galaxy,
invisible curve of the universe,
it is expert on existence:
an all seeing stone eye,
while we are but a wink
in the world's story.

SHE SHORE

Coquette at sunset,
the delicate breakers
are her frilled petticoat's hem;
the wet sand her mirror,
long spoiled with unsilvering.

Her beach boudoir is
littered with laddered weed
like soiled stockings
and the discarded jewellery
of too familiar pebbles.

Recumbent, her spite
is quick to unbridle.
The gulls are her sirens
luring the fishing boats.
She sports them like brooches.

Slipping from shore
she leaves shadowy secrets
in sun-bleached stone:
the worn-smooth bone
of long dead lovers.

BEYOND THE SENSE OF ROAD

The car clambers
a gravelly pass.
We peer out thrilling
at precarious drops.
Small scratches of rain
mark the glass.
A sketchpad sky with
smudged charcoal cloud
rings mountains skirted
in verdigris velvet,
faded, weathered like
stout spinsters, proud
in their crumpled dresses,
Miss Haversham veils.
As still as the dead,
the range stretches out:
the fist of a corpse
towards splash of sails
and rock like bleached bone
worn smooth with strokes,
to breakers flouncing their lace petticoats
where flat sand reflects sky
like the skin of a pearl.
We crawl ever higher
to the top of the world.
Rock bruised from creation
bathes in dusk's fiery silk.
In key-shrouded silence,
we breathe the breath of beginning,
air scented with afterbirth,
as soft cloud spills over us
like mother's milk.

OLD STORIES AND NEW ONES

Another day slides off the sunlit page
dimming like failing torchlight
into a night of uncertainties.
As we sleep, around the world,
breaths puncture the air a final time,
while rosy little lungs fight their way
into a fragile new morning.

CAESAR

For Daniel

The clock's moon face
swallowed another minute,
announced your birthtime:
7.52 (as rush hour trains swelled).
Yanked from my split belly
you must have gulped
your first piece of jagged air.
A shrivelled plum, your alarm
rang sexless through two rooms
to your father.

At 7.53 they must have cut our cord:
the food chain, your pulsating path
back to the old world. Clipped and tagged
like a screaming bird, the cold scales
welcomed your arrival, measured your wholeness.
As I lay in enforced oblivion
(my spirit somewhere grateful for relief)
the bikini wound was mopped
and mended as if in apology:
your birthmark.

Empty of your muffled kicks
at 8.15, unburdened and unbloody,
I was taken half-awake to where you were,
now sexed and swaddled in your father's arms:
a small blue question mark.
Your mouth rooting for
the milky smell of love.
But I slipped away before I held you
and hours lost themselves
until we met.

THE THREAD

Quietly, hovering at your doorway,
I listen for your butterfly breath:
the petal-soft snuffle of the just.
You lie as safe as I can make you:
your downy head like
a tiny chick nested in the thick
of grandma's quilt, your paper
eyelids shut fast and still, trusting
life to grow your tiny spark to flame.
In this star-stung darkness, you are still
no more than smallest piece of star yourself:
a cupid's arrow from the universe.

I linger, do not want to leave,
give up my trust to
a scary scythe-mooned night:
that may safely carry you
into morning's hug or instead
might choose to take you;
steal nine months of
constant carry; spitefully
snap the bonds we stitched
so carefully from your first cry,
when we held your tiny fist,
your fingers an unfurling bud.

I blow a kiss and though it
floats invisible as air,
it's filled to burst with all the love
that's possible to hold: a bubble
wrapped in rainbows, round and fat
as when you were your unborn self.
I have just this: the prayer
that with each night that darkens,
you will share with us tomorrow:
your eyes will open like little worlds;
you will smile, small hands reaching;
your chest breathing.

BOY IN A BOAT

For Elliot

At Charmouth, the river runs out to sea,
forking gently through fossil rocks
past windbreak flotillas
billowing across stony sand.
A tiny sea invites a tiny boat.
He drags the dinghy air made rock
across an obstacle of terrain
to an oasis ringing with chorus semaphored
across a thousand summer seashores.
To watch, the boat might be a man's weight.
He heaves with sun-kissed baby arms,
launches clumsily from a shifting jetty
of microscopic bones, hauls himself horizontal,
belly flops into the bottom like a landed mackerel;
rights himself before taking up the oars, testing them
as he is swallowed by the heliographic throng.

KITE SURFER

Ferocious sea winds take him,
slam his slim brown body like a locomotive,
tossing him leaf-like from the tumbling surf
and sixteen feet to the sky.
Exotic insect he hovers
beneath a striped strip of canvas,
twists with ease, spins ninety degrees,
lands sure-footed and precise
upon the next wave.
He glides it sideways like a piste;
one muscle on a tiny hairpin,
faster than a flickering eye.
Fists of wind punch and yank.
Spiteful waves shove and bite.
He remains in perfect balance
like a little tightrope walker
suspended within his elements.

MENISCUS ACROBAT

It balances between air and water
performing miracles metamorphosis perfected,
its tiny oars dimpling the meniscus,
distorting it lightly like a fairground mirror:
a pencil point pressed upon a plasma screen.

I watch it row in twitching circles,
marvel at its trust of the water's skin, or perhaps
its ignorance of the fathoms below it.

THE PLAYGROUND

We never forget our nine-month sacrifice.
We watch you now, gladly sacrificing still,
as you swing, scream, slide and tumble -
all limbs within the safety of this wire fence:
our communal womb. You wage your high-pitched wars,
cherry-cheeked as cherubs in your scruffy duffle coats
and snowsuits. We wait to mend your scuffed knees,
dab each salty frustration. We are the peacemakers,
anticipating your schemes and strategies.
Huddled blithely on benches with buggies,
we appear impotent, our warm breaths
settling in spiteful air, strung out around
a waiting room of inevitable wants,
confident of our necessity. We ask for nothing
but co-operation. We have learned the value of life;
seen the savage second that may snuff you out.
We have donated ourselves. As you laugh and leap
in a perilous metal world, we know one day
we will lose you, but we preserve and perpetuate.
Other armies will replace us.
We are mother.

INDIAN SUMMER

Lofty in a nest of bramble, its pine poles
leant together like ribs.
Beneath paleface skin, colourful cotton made
the wide floor welcome like patchwork grass.
Inside, safe from wind, plants danced like shadow puppets.

The fathomless pond was an emerald hall,
flicking rainbow trout from its freckled mirror;
blackberries ripened within our purple-fingered reach.

Our calls echoed until dusk when sunset campfires
came alive, smoke-signalling our neighbours;
flames convulsing like dancing spirits
luring us to the potlatch ritual.

Each canvas cone became a paper lantern.
We sat and stared at our small circle of stars,
the centre of a spoked circle: our medicine wheel.

AUTUMN FINDINGS

Close by my foot,
hidden amongst twigs,
a tiny corpse lies dried
like paper on the grass:
earth-matted grey feathers
stuck sparse to bony wings,
yawning songless beak;
sightless eyes; skull,
an ivory bubble bared,
fractured like an eggshell,
the cut of a sharp heel
could crush to dust.
Frail shadow of a bird,
that sung a summer passing,
became a brittle memory.

BIRDSONG

Robin

Midsummer sun grazes my back
as I stretch the brush, dripping,
to the tip of the dry, bleached wood.

Ox-blood stain bleeds into the grain,
feathering out; pearls of perspiration
decorate my forehead.

He flits into the edge of my perception;
perches lightly on the fence blade, full facing me,
close enough to cup; apple-pip eyes as bright

as the scarlet signal of his breast.
Robin and I regard each other, motionless,
he, cock-headed, beak full of green grub,

oddly unafraid, perhaps flattered
by my fence - the colour of his breast - or
in gratitude for breakfast crusts.

Eye-to-eye, we speak across the space
between our species; he is a tiny question mark
jotted in the margin of my labour.

Life's too quick, he says. With
a feathered flourish he returns to summer
in a joyful ruby wink.

Barn Owl

Moonlight makes my gatepost centre stage
where a ghost with marble amber eyes sits silently,
his face a satellite dish turned three-sixty degrees.

Good evening, my name is *Tyto Alba*, he says.
I live by my ears but you will not hear me coming.
I am the sudden whisper in the field. I am death's white messenger.

If you are small, I will steal your life breath. Fear me.
And he stretches a wingspan, screeches like a banshee,
swoops low and soundless across the garden, back to the
Otherworld.

Blackbird

Son of four and twenty,
ebony, gold-rimmed and tipped,
lover and master of verse and song,
you jealously guard the garden
as your own all seasons long.

Turdus merula, lover of fruits
whose dun mate lays early speckled
topaz treasure in low hedgerows,
still chattering past bedtime,
first rising when horizon glows.

Condemner of cats, braveheart,
constant to his love in her untidy nest,
anywhere dweller, flyer of night,
Jack the lad who might just be tamed
if the price were right.

Song Thrush

Fat and freckle-chested in my shallow sparkled stream
he sits, wings panting, tips trailed across the cooled sun splinters.
Betraying bliss, his eyes are glossy beetles, constantly surveying
for the sinister movement. No leave from death watch.

He is the firework in negative: a riot of dark sparks;
frenzied musical notes on a yellowing page
penned long ago by a genius composer; his songs
are a medley of tsips. Proud of his garden repertoire,

he puffs and shimmers. Once bathed, he will hop lightly,
bone-dry from the water, tilt-headed and ready to search for shells.
In the woodpile, he may find a snail. Conchologist, he will
claim it quickly in his scissor beak, dissect it upon the stones.

Starlings

They jostle one another
out of the sky: the squabbling
scavenge for the bare bones
of bread we abandon to them.
Strutting in tatty jackets like
noisy miniature fighting cocks,
sparrows flee in their wake.
They are all untidiness,
feathers black and iridescent
as if dipped in dirty oil,
preening *braggadocios*.
Sated, they depart in groups
to fidget in the sycamore,
heckling, spoiling for a fight.

Wren

She was tiny in his sharp mouth:
a crumpled fascinator,
crushed, unmoving,
giving up her right to life.
He dropped her gently when I asked.

She seemed unharmed until I saw
the sticky tell-tale trickle at the neck.
Her head flopped but a minute eye
blinked black and glistening,
beak open, panting: just a baby.

I scooped her quickly and she lay,
soft feathered treasure in my palm:
helpless, forced to trust, awaiting judgement
while he blankly watched.
I searched vainly for the hidden nest,

close to ground; crept around
her mother's chatters of alarm
with quiet words of comfort,
marvelling at her small perfection:
heart-stopping miracle of creation;

a shadow of life, so easily taken.
Could I dare snuff out her suffering?
And in that hopeless moment, she stirred,
slowly curled her foot around my finger

and she flew.

Pigeons

In the streaked fire of a dusk-lit sky
hovering at the edge of winter,
our eyes at rest on the twig-fringed horizon,
we watched them fall, first one, then many:
a spinning descent of unfathomable snowflakes
or air-blown ash from a distant bonfire.

Pigeon hundreds dropping softly
to meet the field in a forage of ecstasy,
feathered blizzard that ceased suddenly when
wings whipped upwards into a thunderous squall,
masked for a moment the disintegrating sky
to vanish into the backdrop, waiting for the next fall.

REQUIEM FOR A DAWN CHORUS

I miss it still: that first crescendous twittering of light,
chattering celebration of dawn rising
to riotous welcome as if, like Aztecs,
they doubted the myth of its return.

And I, who was born late,
on the edge of the end
never imagined then
the miracle of those early years
shared with a fragile fleeting
fragment of time like
a blackbird's blue freckled egg
in a child's hand.

Another deaf London dawn limps in
with the shadows of forgotten things
unprecious until lost forever.

CORNWALL

I dreamed of taking you to Cornwall when winter light
slides its fingers between harboured fishing boats
and slate roofs huddle beneath the hush of rain.

I dreamed we walked the pebbled streets,
worn with the memory of a thousand summer footsteps,
past shuttered shops, grey gulls crying their despair.

I dreamed of wind-snatched words on the cold whipped beach,
the rough rush of sea like a hymn to solitude,
big enough to share and empty of other voices.

I dreamed of you and I together in a tiny room,
grey light leaking in through the rattling shuttered window
and our bodies enough for warmth.

SELLING THE WIND

And then the witch spoke:
"Sailor come buy
this three-knotted rope
blessed by my third eye.
Its magic is your hope
of winds and fair sky.

"The first knot fills your sails,
the second blows gales
and the third is a tempest."

Inspired by an old Cornish proverb

THE ROSE

I overlooked the blushing daisy,
instead, deconstructed the rose,
counting each dusk-kissed pearly petal
as it drifted down to stroke the floor:

He loves me,
He loves me not,
He loves me,
He loves me not,
He loves me.

I forgot the blues of the forget-me-not,
instead, gently wrote a syncopated love note
on every soft-lipped satin heart
to launch skywards and shower him
in some invisible future,
like a dream of confetti.

INSIDE LOVE

He is engraved onto her soul,
soldered to her spirit. He
lights sparklers in her heart
until stars fizz inside her chest
and fill her throat. She cannot speak

of love or anything. The longing lasts
with small relief in sleep although
her dreams still fill with him.
It is a sickness, heavy-lidded,
fingers tingling for his touch.

Her breath becomes shallow
waiting for the deep intake
she'll allow in his first kiss.
She is becoming his mirror
by fragments, losing herself.

GLOVES

I have had erotic thoughts
of gloves: the velvet-fingered
stroke unseen beneath your shirt;
of leather gloves held paired
to sting a gasp against your skin,
their tannin scent the echo of a beast;
gloves of silky rubber stretched
as taut as Clingfilm, oiled to slide.
If Freud's gloves were vaginas,
I am glistening satin: wear me.
And as a glove recalls
its owner's hand, I will fit
the measure of you.

SONG OF THE UNIVERSE

I am a shimmering melody in the half light.
Touch me slowly, unwind my breath
into the song of the universe.

I am alive with sparkles, the echo of stars
stretched languidly across the silky night.
Play me like a soft prelude to your pleasure

the notes rising and falling: pianissimo,
staccato, forte - reaching up for that sweet
unbearable sunburst crescendo.

SEPTEMBER

I think of you as September leaves appear;
the autumn photograph develops high above my head.
I cannot imagine a winter without you.

The sky bathes in a sun of lost ferociousness;
filled with the lead shot of migrating birds
sensing new horizons.

I am forever driving, swallowing road:
a voiceless face within the windscreen,
never really arriving.

I think of you living your life without thought of me
and wish that I could be just a tiny part
like an ant that walks across your footstep.

AFTER THE DINNER PARTY

She should have guessed,
adjusted her depth of field,
looked properly through her wine glass.

She recalls them laughing,
overripe smiles split like swollen cherries,
sipped glances with their Sangiovese.

While she laid the dishes tenderly
with rare Beef Wellington,
oblivious in its pastry bed

they were under the table
rutting like the neighbour's cats.
She never noticed.

"Would you like more sauce?"
It was the lingering touch
of farewell fingers at the door.

It was the simple note
scratched on a napkin and discarded,
reckless in the lust:

Call me tomorrow.

Sitting amidst fragments
of bone china, blood congealing
on the oven door

she poured herself another gin.

DEATH'S ACRE

Let me lay
you here
my love
beneath

these bowers
of sky
pallid
reflection

of your face
leaf shadows
across your brow

dead now
and buried
secret
in this copse

you will dissolve
and melt
into the roots

of this black oak.

THE LAST NEGATIVE

The final film roll of our years
will develop into a past of prints
pegged out, fixed in tears, and shut
inside the darkroom of memory.

As an indifferent world turns the album page,
our story will fade like an ageing Polaroid,
moments not displayed; a strip of silver negatives
cut and trapped in frozen frames.

Our fingers never learned to grasp the digital,
became unclasped, long before
the perfect Instagram, when the
shutter clicked mechanically one final time.

IN THE BOOKSHOP

You were a felled tree, brittle with winter.
I caught the sharp snap of your skull
on the spiteful floor, shattering your
spun-glass angel hair, pigment
pick-pocketed by time. You were
scuffed moleskin, a bruised jacket,
Velcro shoes that twitched once
in the tide between your legs.
Songs of Christmas past replayed,
faces turned the other cheek,
stepped shuttered over
your bleached eyes gaping,
purpling skin, wasted mouth set in
silent protest at indignity,
ignorance, the misjudged;
gifts spewed from your bag
like a guilty secret.
Inside the fleshy minutes of
emergencies, your narrow breath spanned
mini eternities, my hands limp as landed fish,
slippery with impotence to mend you:
a broken Beswick, butter-fingered.
When the cocoon of sirens came,
we each slipped into the dark, swallowed
by the pulse of lights, cacophony,
cold crush and shove of carrier bags,
goodwill that cradled someone unaware
you would not be home for Christmas.

A VIEW FROM ST MARY'S

I once rented a view: sunset on a silky
crinkled harbour spread with acquiescent boats
like jacks spilt across a playground.

On the hill, cottages receded into dusk until
tiny windows pierced the dark like angry insects
and the rain advanced.

A predator's shadow, crouched on the horizon
watched a boat depart, its crown a single light
to fish 'in peril on the sea'.

A dapple-grey rowing boat, oars safely inside,
bucked at its rope as a cloud battalion charged
upon the drowsy islands.

Invading quiet skies, the storm raised its roar,
raged a short lifespan. Calm brought forgetfulness.
The sleepy rowing boat, oars tucked

inside its belly, nodded on its rope.
Time darkened. Like a ghost behind my eyelids,
the image floated momentarily, faded and was gone.

THE DISAPPEARED

Now I notice the blue of forget-me-nots, listen
to winds for word of you, my eyes scraping each horizon
for a sign - white feather swinging gently down, surprise sun prism,
each raindrop mirroring the soft tear click of my eyelids.
Nothing comes. Not yet.

This hope is my life raft when the days become myopic.
I threw away my watch when marking time
became like cutting notches in my skin
so, I forget the hours, keep my focus upon nothing
but the day that is not here.

I wash your empty plate each morning, lay your place,
smooth the sheets that loved you sleeping, keep close
your favourite jumper's scent; wait for your familiar footfall
and when night comes I lie, arms outstretched,
always facing the open doorway.

STUDY OF A TEARDROP

Its
tension
trembles
in meniscus:
fragile skin; saline
pear drop snailing south
across a cheek; emotional
essence squeezed out of a soul
window; note of longing, sorrow,
anger, joy, all written within in
invisible ink; it is the sound byte
of silence held inside the sob;
the much unsaid imprinted
upon water; like a solitary
silicon chip, deleted
with a finger's
single dab.

THE SLOW DIVE

I sink into the dead place:
black water where no light touches,
not even a shallow thread can enter.
There is not a single moth hole:
I sewed them all, tight as a tourniquet.

My vista is all stones and monochrome:
charcoal and ash. It is the end of Pompei;
cloud tent of Hiroshima. I did not choose
to be here, snagging inside unwanted flesh,
chief witness of the meaningless.

I am set like a compass at the opposite pole to
the midnight sun, deep within the bowels
of an oubliette; dropped and squeezed carelessly
through the waste pipe; stricken by amnesia of sunlight.
Today, I am the black dog in the depth of the slow dive.

LITTLE CAGE

A tiny bird sings behind the wires.
She knows no other language, desires
only to fill air's silence.

She is the weight of a soul suspended
in the metal cage around her,
bright sunshine casting bars
upon her wings, as if even light
conspired in her capture.
Who knows what she sings for?

Freedom's longing, rapture
at the blue beyond, or for
unconditional love of her imprisoner?

SUGAR THIEF

He flits in low
        bat-shadow a blink could miss,
           sucrologist; pincher finch
slipping through the light's gash.
    He knows the confines of this room,
       airborne, negotiates its edges:
ace in a tumbling *Tiger Moth*
    slick with sharp manoeuvres;
       a feathered compass.
North is the white prize, its chemistry tattooed on his DNA
    here where the Caribbean polishes the sand to pink.
       Where rainforest was hobbled for molasses
his ancestors sneaked into windmills to scoop cane droplets,
    swooped through bagasse smoke,
       braved boiling houses.
Hollow-boned strongman
    he lifts the packet equal to his weight.
       Showing off his blood throat,
with his dangling prize
    he is like a stork with a baby,
       bold as rum punch.
The chinagraph skin is easy to pierce, tissue-thin;
    his shiny eyes challenge,
       tiny as tamarind seeds.
In short swift jerks, he disembowels his prize
    owns the four grams of sweetness
       that have become his birth right.

CANOUAN

Petite Grenadine, *lune de miel*,
you are bittersweet with memory.
Shadow island at sunset, by day
your ocean shimmered with scales.
The lustrous lizard on the lock
we nicknamed Lizzie, laughing;
the huge horseshoe crabs that
nightly rattled at our door:
the forgotten obstacle;
the white-hot beach begging
for sea breezes; slow catamaran
with fat sails set somewhere west
for other islands and lure of fish;
the lazy hours spent floating
on the flashing sun-glint tide
when time slid over the side of the boat;
the shoals of squid, goggle-eyed and
glowing in the half-beam ocean light,
fleeing from our rusty breathing.
The sun, a stop bath on our skin,
developed us like the photographs
we keep within an album layered
beneath two decades of dust.

SLEEPLESSNESS

I lie on my back, eyes open
and the duvet rests gently
against my bones like
your echo on my skin.
You are next to me
but drifted away across
the wide water of dreams.
The half-light makes the world
turn grey, and I hear
your breath, the ticking clock,
and watch the paleness of your back
until the dawn cracks open.

THE ARCHITECT OF MOTHS

My bathroom light becomes their moon
luring them in like tiny drunken paper bats
to hurl headlong against the ceiling.

Geometry unimagined by man
in infinite shades of only brown:
freckled velvet, silvered satin, furry.

Who conceived their triangles; measured
with universal compass, set square,
acute angles, the obtuse, oblique, isosceles, equilateral?

Who constructed their elaborate 3D wing plans;
sketched bodies like box kites, antennae equations,
and fathomless eyes of compound circles?

Professor of maths and perfect proportion,
entomologist, exoskeleton expert, lover
of light and lightness, methodical lunatic.

The Architect of Moths, who made their blueprints,
shook powder over ink-wet wings to dry,
and gently blew brief night life into them.

SKIPPING STONES

I whisk past your ear but you do not hear me
until I hit the lake top, bounce two times and drop.
To you I am a splash in water that perhaps
reminds you of the school yard swim: a plunge
into the icy clasp of a first term morning.

I watch you enviously live your life above the water,
open my mouth to speak to you and only bubbles rise
as silent as a pebble spun across the still pond where
you never see below the surface or remember
that I lie there, dreaming of my perfect flatness in your palm.

THE MEMORY OF SNOW

Our faces glittered with cold
as we raced the mountain to its edge,
skis hissing on the sparkle:
sugar white, deep as December's kiss.
Tiny stars twinkled on our collar as
we set up the rhythm like a dance of love,
swaying frosted pine-fringed pistes,
we cut the wavy line: our signature
upon the crisp white page.
We were air angels then, without wanting,
content to fly beneath a brittle sky
as if we could soar for eternity.

FIREWORKS

Hunched into coat's glow,
hands thrust into
misshapen pockets, noses
nipped, cheeks numb,
eyes catching fire crackle,
we watch each string of gleams
rip into the dark.

Night uncoils hissing, fills with steam,
colour cavalcades upon colour,
bursts in feathers, peacock plumes,
shrieking sparks, lancing
burnt javelins until charred skies
billow sailboats of smoke,
the smell of ash in burnished air.

We are the witnesses,
hundreds of us, chattering,
gasping, pointing, sighing
as each brilliant creation
burns out its glory in a final scream,
snuffed from existence,
leaving our world in darkness.

ORIGAMI

Now I wake each day
to the assassin's creep,
cruel cold stab at
the quiet conceit
of everlasting youth.
Heralded by disappointment,
the first faint line,
crow intruder footprints,
cracks in perfect flesh,
shock flash of grey.
Betrayal begins.
Hollows appear
in skin once plump-ripe.
Convex turns to concave.
Features melt and migrate,
plum becomes prune.
Paper folding.

Inside I am myself
Of forty summers-plus but
I have learned to turn
in mirrors towards
the angle of acceptance.
I have come to love candlelight.
And in photographs
I no longer recognise myself.
I forget the face I was.
Old age brings the stranger.

CHURCHYARD CHILDREN

A mire of memories moulders here.
Mouthless, they cannot taste
our ripening summer, nor feel
this beckoning bell's cool thud
made dim by their mossy shrouds.
Their eyes are all dust.
Warped by time, and time-oblivious,
the dark boxes wither
their limbs like leaves.
Laughter, caresses, love and kisses
are flotsam upon some shadowy sea.
Stones seem superfluous.
Nodding grass is their epitaph.
Our Sundays go on.
Six feet and eternity separate us.

SNOWMAN

At autumn's end
when snow muffled
and made mute
the last leaves' whisperings,
dressed trees in shrouds, buried
dead ground in a coffin of ice,
you sickened slowly
in a solitary, white room.
Your cheeks hollowed,
grey as sky; your eyes
frosted and your old
freckled arms withered;
your legs, blanketed,
brittle, light as twigs.

At winter's peak
when rivers froze,
you ceased.
The thaw came,
wept at the snowman's death.
Left, leaving no trace.

FINAL NOTES OF A BOY (ON EXPEDITION TO THE CAIRNGORMS)

There is no shelter,
only the barren outcrops of ice-tipped rock
and jagged sheets of purple stone
jutting like prehistoric blades
through the frozen soles of our boots.
The snow-capped wind splinters our bones.
When the vast climb gets steep,
it presses our numb raw cheeks
against the vertical. Exhausted
we cannot sleep for shivering
while the wind jabs ceaselessly
at our Polaris.

There is no shelter,
not anywhere.
None of us imagined this,
not at the border.
Not at base camp.

Mac is relentless.
He says we must push on.
No rest.
Not now.
He thinks we'll make it.
Time, I think
is running out.

MUNTJAC

We would glimpse your rustling,
clumsy shot of russet cracking,
irritating leaves: a bonsai creature.
You left your mark, frayed cloven prints
disguised in earth, nibbled plants,
your shadow touching every twilight.
That night I caught you in my headlights,
sitting on the verge, head bowed.
You had never let me touch you.
Your chest heaved heavy with tyre tracks.
My torch caught the red saliva glint
across the tarmac, a tough little antler
torn away. They were distracted,
young, too fast. I stole the time
to stroke your chipped worn hide,
knowing it would not be warm for long.
Your wide eyes slowly turned to mildewed conkers.
I stayed with you until night and nature
could do nothing but to take you back.

THE OLDEST TANNERY IN MARRAKECH

'You are welcome' he said, bowed his head, gave us mint leaves,
beckoned. Stench swallowed us like rancid breath:
wet dog, slurry, butcher's block, acrid detritus of the dead,
disturbingly familiar, snagging at each intake's edge.

He pointed to where a dozen stone wells, aged as him, were filled
with brownish suppurating soup: depilatory remains.
"Pigeon *sheet*" he said, face creasing like his leather;
pyrographed with all the tanning secrets of his fathers.

Flayed sheets flapped in the gritty breeze, strung out
like serial trophies, ready to dye. In a tumbledown shed,
where women sewed unseen, we walked past weeping donkeys
to an emporium of the useful dead, all stitched together.

THE ROUTE TO DA NANG

For Sergeant Wes Caton, US Air Force, Vietnam from 1955-75

Forty summers past you were Dante's Charon,
airborne, your eyes locked on the remote outpost:
not site of the hill fights, but for you, Hades;
unhappy guardian of Khe Sanh; ruler of silence
while corpses death rattled in the cargo hold.
The still warm breath in their mouth was their only coin,
as you flew out across Acheron, the River Styx, your
heart heavy in the fuselage, to the only certainty.

THE SPIRIT'S PLAYHOUSE

When we find it
the glass box is silent:
wheels do not turn,
bells hang damped,
empty of ectoplasm.
In a past when its spirits
were perhaps familiar
it was crafted carefully,
the curious lure
for a mischievous soul:
terrarium playhouse
of tiny toys for those without
and that within.
Now its present is empty.
But for a spirit
with eternity to kill,
a nap might just
last a century.

During Victorian times, it was popular to make 'spirit houses' - a glass box filled with bells and wheels meant to trap a ghost and keep it occupied inside, thus providing entertainment for the living. Years ago, before the terrible 2004 floods, I saw one at the Museum of Witchcraft in Boscastle, Cornwall and it inspired this poem.

POPPIES

I write crimson poetry
from a dark heart.
Blooming the petals blow,
seeds scatter where they please.
More poppies grow.

PREVIOUSLY PUBLISHED

Churchyard Children	*Pause*, The National Poetry Foundation magazine, 1993
She Shore	*Pause*, The National Poetry Foundation magazine, 1994
Final Notes of a Boy	*Inspirations from Central England*, Anchor Books, 1995
Caesar	*The Stages of Life*, Anchor Books, 1998
Beyond the Sense of Road	*Inspirations from Central England*, Anchor Books, 1998 and *The Best of 2005 – The Winchester Writers' Silver Jubilee Conference*
Snowman	*Mildew and Mandarins*, Seafield Publishing, 2002
The Playground	*Bright Voices*, United Press, 2003
A View from St Mary's	*National Poetry Anthology 2004*, United Press
Inside Love	*Affectionately Yours*, United Press, 2005
The Memory of Snow	*Poetic Images*, Poetry in Print, 2005
Origami	*Reach* magazine, March 2006
Carrion Crow	*Reach* magazine, May 2006
September	*Island Dreams*, Poetry in Print, 2006
Ammonite	*Reach* magazine, September 2006
The Rose	Reach magazine, November 2006 and *The New Poetry – In Love*, Copeland Books, 2009

Published as Catherine Rose

AWARDS AND COMMENDATIONS

September 1974	Third prize in the Brent Literary Children's Short Story Competition.
September 2008	Runner up in the *Impulse* love poetry competition judged by Brian Patten.
September 2003	Shortlisted for United Press 2004 National Poetry Competition.
May 2005	First prize in the *Winchester Writers' Conference* Poetry Competition – Reaching Out sponsored by Penguin Books.
May 2005	Highly commended in the *Winchester Writers' Conference* First Chapter of a Children's Novel competition.
January 2006	Shortlisted for Poetry in Print's National Open Poetry Competition.
January 2006	Highly commended in the *Writers' Forum* magazine poetry competition for After the Dinner Party.
October 2007	Second prize in the *Winchester Writers' Conference* First Chapter of a Children's Novel competition.
March 2017	Highly commended for The Spirit House in *The A3 Review*'s Playhouse competition.

www.ingramcontent.com/pod-product-compliance
Ingram Content Group UK Ltd.
Pitfield, Milton Keynes, MK11 3LW, UK
UKHW042004230426
12048UKWH00009B/538

9 781787 195059